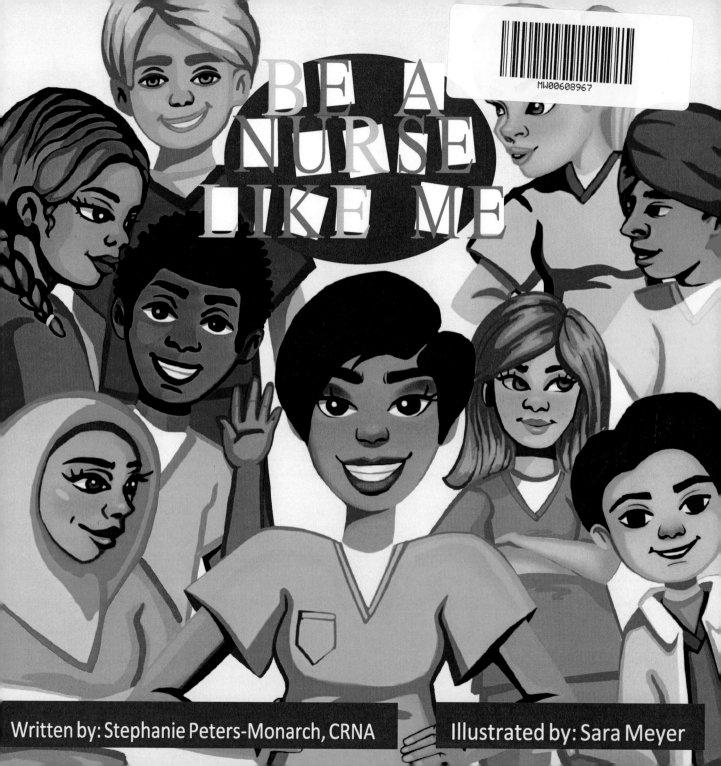

BE A NURSE LIKE ME

Written by: Stephanie Peters-Monarch, CRNA   Illustrated by: Sara Meyer

Acknowledgements

This book is dedicated to all the hard working and fearless nurses, who unselfishly give their all caring for others daily. Thank you for being a
" Nurse Like Me"!

In loving Memory of my Sister LaToya Lynette
I love you forever.

Meet The Author

Stephanie Peters-Monarch is a Certified Registered Nurse Anesthetist (CRNA). Prior to this, she obtained her Bachelor of Science in Nursing (BSN) in 1994 at the age of 20. She worked as a Registered Nurse in many different areas of the Nursing profession. Her favorite areas were ER, OR and ICU nurs - ing. She went on to complete her Master's of Science in Nurse Anesthesia in 2005, after 32 months of clinical and didactic studies.

Becoming a Nurse can be a lot of fun!

Did you know that nurses are here to provide comfort to patients?

What do you think can be fun about being a nurse?

Would you like to be a Nurse Like Me?

_____

_____

_____

_____

_____

_____

_____

_____

_____

_____

_____

_____

_____

_____

I like to teach patients how to take care of themselves and not get sick by exercising and eating fresh fruits and vegetables. Be a nurse like me. I am a Nurse Educator.

If you like to teach, you can be a Nurse Educator!

Did you know that nurses can help you understand how your body works?

What would you like to teach a patient on how to stay healthy?

Would you like to be a Nurse Educator like me?

_____

_____

_____

_____

_____

_____

_____

_____

_____

_____

_____

_____

If you like helping patients after an injury become active again, you can be a Rehabilitation (or Rehab) Nurse!

Did you know nurses are there to help you heal?

What can be an example of something you can do to help a patient heal like a Rehab Nurse?

Would you like to be a Rehab Nurse like me?

_____

_____

_____

_____

_____

_____

_____

_____

_____

_____

_____

If you like seeing newborn babies come into the world, you would love being a Labor and Delivery Nurse!

Did you know that nurses help keep moms comfortable when they are having babies?

Would you like to be a Labor and Delivery Nurse like me?

_____

_____

_____

_____

_____

_____

_____

_____

_____

_____

_____

_____

_____

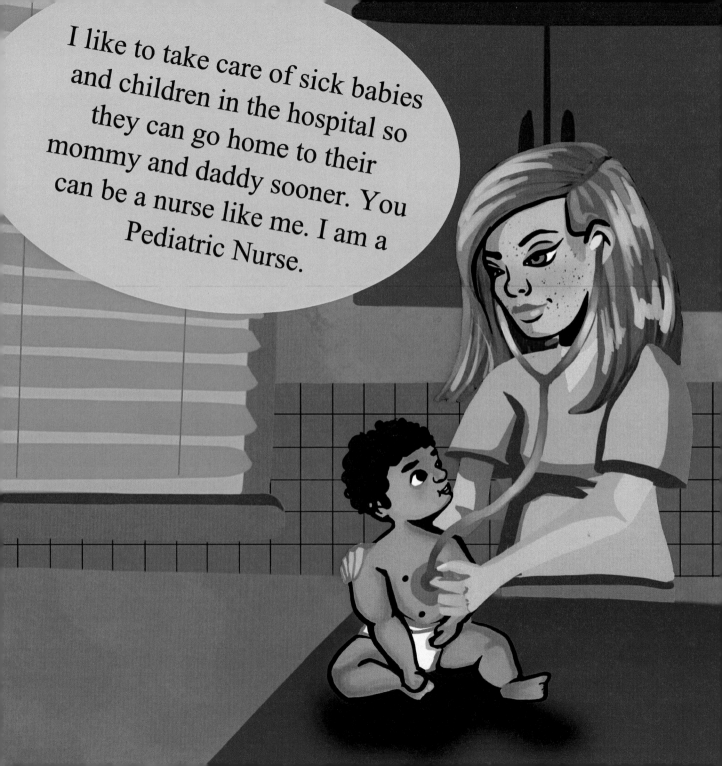

If you have a loving personality and want to help sick children get better, you should become a Pediatric Nurse!

Pediatric nurses become very close to their patients due to the time spent in the hospital.

Did you know that nurses can help make the hospital stay less scary?

Would you like to be a Pediatric Nurse like me?

_____

_____

_____

_____

_____

_____

_____

_____

_____

_____

_____

_____

If you can think fast and move quickly to help save patients coming into the Emergency Room (or ER), you can be an ER Nurse!

Did you know nurses help save lives in an emergency?

Do you think you would like to become an Emergency Room nurse?

An ER nurse is one of the author's favorite type of nursing.

Would you like to be an ER nurse like me?

_____

_____

_____

_____

_____

_____

_____

_____

_____

_____

_____

_____

If you like to fly and help critical patients get to the hospital faster, you can become a Flight Nurse!

How cool is that? Flight Nurses must love to fly and take care of really sick patients.

Would you like to become a Flight Nurse like me?

_____

_____

_____

_____

_____

_____

_____

_____

_____

_____

_____

_____

_____

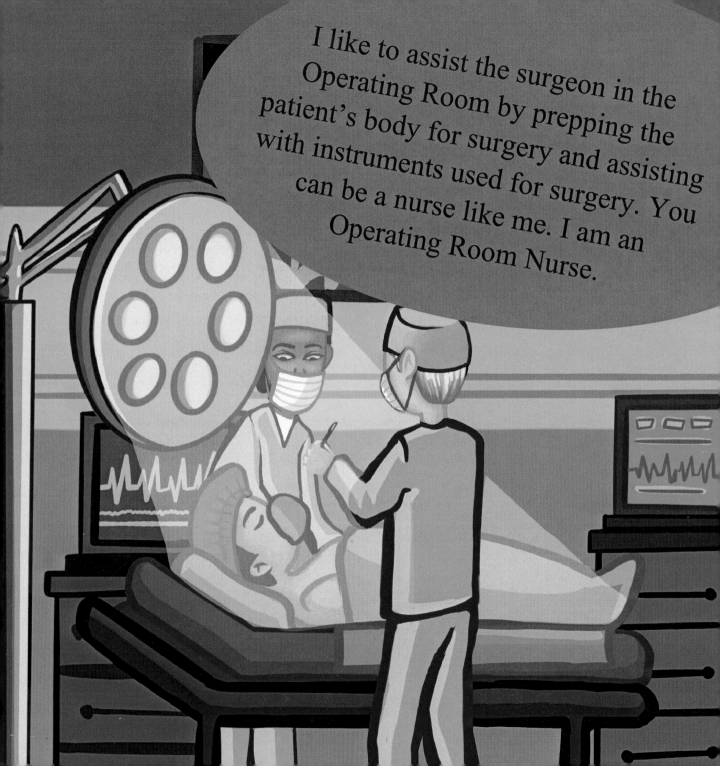

If you like to help in the Operating Room (or OR) with a patient's surgery, you can be an OR Nurse!

Did you know an OR nurse has to learn special instruments and highly technical equipment to make sure the patient's surgery goes well?

Would you like to become an Operating Room Nurse like me?

_____

_____

_____

_____

_____

_____

_____

_____

_____

_____

_____

_____

If you like to put a patient to sleep for surgery and make sure they are safe, you can be a Certified Registered Nurse Anesthetist (or CRNA)!

The author of this book is a Certified Registered Nurse Anesthetist. Did you know that CRNAs monitor and maintain all patients' vital signs while the surgeon does the surgery? How cool is that?

Would you like to become a Certified Registered Nurse Anesthetist like me?

_____

_____

_____

_____

_____

_____

_____

_____

_____

_____

If you like to examine and treat all different kinds of patients, you can be an Advanced Nurse Practitioner!

Nurse Practitioners can specialize in the type of care they give.

Wow! How cool can that be for you?

Did you know nurses are friends who care about what happens to you?

Would you like to be an Advanced Nurse Practitioner like me?

_____

_____

_____

_____

_____

_____

_____

_____

_____

_____

_____

Glossary

Nurse- A person educated and trained to care for the sick in a hospital and non-hospital settings.

Nurse Educator- A nurse educator is a nurse who teaches and prepares students to become Registered Nurses (***RN***). Also, they provide or educate patients in a hospital setting to improve their health.

Rehabilitation Nurse- A nurse who specializes in helping patients move towards being able to take care of themselves after being sick.

Labor and Delivery Nurse- A nurse who helps mothers while they are carrying their babies and helps them with the birth (delivery) of the newborn child. They assist the doctor with all parts of the delivery.

Pediatric Nurse- A nurse that takes care of newborn babies and children in the hospital.

Emergency Room Nurse- (ER Nurse)- a nurse that works in the emergency department cares for patients in unexpected sickness in any form.

Flight Nurse- a nurse that has advanced training in emergency and critical care to help make stable a very sick patient and help transport to the hospital.

Operating Room Nurse- (OR nurse)- a nurse who learns each operation and knows how to assist the surgeon on each procedure. An OR nurse learns each instrument for the surgery. They also assist in caring for the patient in the operating room.

Certified Registered Nurse Anesthetist- (CRNA)- a nurse with an advanced education and training who puts patients to sleep for all types of surgeries in many different settings.

Advanced Practice Nurse- (APN)- a nurse with an advanced education and training that can assist doctors in managing and taking care of sick patients in the community and hospital.

Made in United States
North Haven, CT
26 April 2022

18614573R00015